ENT KIND CREATIVE OUTSPOKEN SMART INCLUSIVE
E ARTISTIC DETERMINED RESILIENT KIND CREATIVE
RING POETIC BRAVE INVENTIVE ARTISTIC DETERMINED
SIVE LOVING THOUGHTFUL DARING POETIC BRAVE
REATIVE OUTSPOKEN SMART INCLUSIVE LOVING
DETERMINED RESILIENT KIND CREATIVE OUTSPOKEN
BRAVE INVENTIVE ARTISTIC DETERMINED RESILIENT
OUGHTFUL DARING POETIC BRAVE INVENTIVE ARTISTIC
ART INCLUSIVE LOVING THOUGHTFUL DARING POETIC
D CREATIVE OUTSPOKEN SMART INCLUSIVE LOVING
DETERMINED RESILIENT KIND CREATIVE OUTSPOKEN
BRAVE INVENTIVE ARTISTIC DETERMINED RESILIENT
OUGHTFUL DARING POETIC BRAVE INVENTIVE ARTISTIC
ART INCLUSIVE LOVING THOUGHTFUL DARING POETIC
D CREATIVE OUTSPOKEN SMART INCLUSIVE LOVING
DETERMINED RESILIENT KIND CREATIVE OUTSPOKEN
BRAVE INVENTIVE ARTISTIC DETERMINED RESILIENT
OUGHTFUL DARING POETIC BRAVE INVENTIVE ARTISTIC
ART INCLUSIVE LOVING THOUGHTFUL DARING POETIC
D CREATIVE OUTSPOKEN SMART INCLUSIVE LOVING

Running Press Kids
Hachette Book Group
1290 Avenue of the Americas, New York, NY 10104
www.runningpress.com/rpkids
@RP_Kids

Printed in China

First Edition: August 2022

Published by Running Press Kids, an imprint of Perseus Books, LLC, a subsidiary of Hachette Book Group, Inc.
The Running Press Kids name and logo is a trademark of the Hachette Book Group.

The Hachette Speakers Bureau provides a wide range of authors for speaking events.
To find out more, go to www.hachettespeakersbureau.com or call (866) 376-6591.

The publisher is not responsible for websites (or their content) that are not owned by the publisher.

Interior and cover illustrations by Cheryl Thuesday.
Print book cover and interior design by Marissa Raybuck.

Library of Congress Cataloging-in-Publication Data
Names: Prager, Sarah, 1986- author. | Thuesday, Cheryl, illustrator.
Title: Kind like Marsha : learning from LGBTQ+ leaders / written by Sarah Prager ; illustrated by Cheryl "Ras" Thuesday.
Description: First edition. | New York, NY : Running Press Kids, 2022. | Audience: Ages: 4-8
Identifiers: LCCN 2021002914 (print) | LCCN 2021002915 (ebook) | ISBN 9780762475001 (hardcover) | ISBN 9780762474998 (ebook) |
ISBN 9780762475018 (ebook) | ISBN 9780762475254 (ebook) | ISBN 9780762475261 (ebook)
Subjects: LCSH: Sexual minorities--Biography--Juvenile literature.
Classification: LCC HQ75.2 .P74 2022  (print) | LCC HQ75.2  (ebook) | DDC  306.76092/2 [B]--dc23
LC record available at https://lccn.loc.gov/2021002914
LC ebook record available at https://lccn.loc.gov/2021002915

ISBNs: 978-0-7624-7500-1 (hardcover), 978-0-7624-7525-4 (ebook),
978-0-7624-7499-8 (ebook), 978-0-7624-7526-1 (ebook)

1010

10  9  8  7  6  5  4  3  2  1

# KIND LIKE MARSHA

## LEARNING FROM LGBTQ+ LEADERS

Written by **Sarah Prager**

Illustrated by **Cheryl "Ras" Thuesday**

RP|KIDS

PHILADELPHIA

# MARSHA P. JOHNSON

**(1945–1992, United States)**

......................

You can be KIND like Marsha.

Marsha P. Johnson was an activist who took care of everyone in her community in New York City.

"PAY IT NO MIND."

ACTUP

# HARVEY MILK

## (1930–1978, United States)

......................

You can be INCLUSIVE like Harvey.

Harvey Milk brought people together for the cause of equality by talking about respecting everyone even if they were different.

> "HOPE WILL NEVER BE SILENT."

CASTRO CAMERA

# SAPPHO

## (c. 610–c. 570 BCE, Greece)

......................

You can be **EXPRESSIVE** like Sappho.

Sappho was a woman who wrote
love poems about other women
more than two thousand years ago!

**"ONE DAY THEY'LL REMEMBER US."**

# X GONZÁLEZ

**(b. 1999, United States)**

..................

You can be OUTSPOKEN like X.

**X González is an activist who organizes millions of people and speaks out about making schools safer for everyone.**

"IT'S TIME TO START DOING SOMETHING."

# LEONARDO DA VINCI

**(1452–1519, Italy)**

......................

**You can be CREATIVE like Leonardo.**

Leonardo da Vinci invented so many cool creations. He made a robot, a scuba suit, and even a helicopter!

> "LEARNING NEVER EXHAUSTS THE MIND."

# SYLVIA RIVERA

**(1951–2002, United States)**

........................

You can be DETERMINED like Sylvia.

Sylvia Rivera was an activist who defended her community, even when people told her to stop.

> "WE HAVE TO BE VISIBLE."

# FRANK MUGISHA

**(b. 1979, Uganda)**

..................

You can be BRAVE like Frank.

Frank Mugisha fights for equal rights
for LGBTQ+ people in Uganda, where
it is illegal to be LGBTQ+.

> "WE WILL NOT GIVE UP UNTIL WE HAVE
> THE FUTURE WE ALL DESERVE."

# AUDRE LORDE

## (1934–1992, United States)

..................

You can be THOUGHTFUL like Audre.

Audre Lorde wrote about equal rights for women, Black people, and gay people. She turned her thoughts about justice into writing that made others change their minds.

"WE ARE POWERFUL BECAUSE
WE HAVE SURVIVED."

# AI OF HAN

## (27–1 BCE, China)

.....................

You can be **LOVING** like Ai.

Emperor Ai of Han ruled all of China,
but he always made time for the man
he loved the most: Dong Xian.

"I KNOW YOUR FAITHFULNESS."

# FRIDA KAHLO

## (1907–1954, Mexico)

........................

You can be ARTISTIC like Frida.

Frida Kahlo created beautiful paintings that often showed herself (sometimes with cute animals). She was proud of who she was.

> "I AM HAPPY TO BE ALIVE AS LONG AS I CAN PAINT."

# LYNN CONWAY

## (b. 1938, United States)

.....................

You can be SMART like Lynn.

Lynn Conway helped make the little computers that are used inside all electronic devices (like tablets and phones) today.

> "IT'S THE LEARNING THAT'S FUN."

# ALBERTO SANTOS-DUMONT

**(1873–1932, Brazil/France)**

.....................

## You can be DARING like Alberto.

Alberto Santos-Dumont created some of the first-ever airplanes and other flying machines. Even when the airships would crash (with him inside), he'd keep trying again and again.

> "STILL I PERSEVERED."

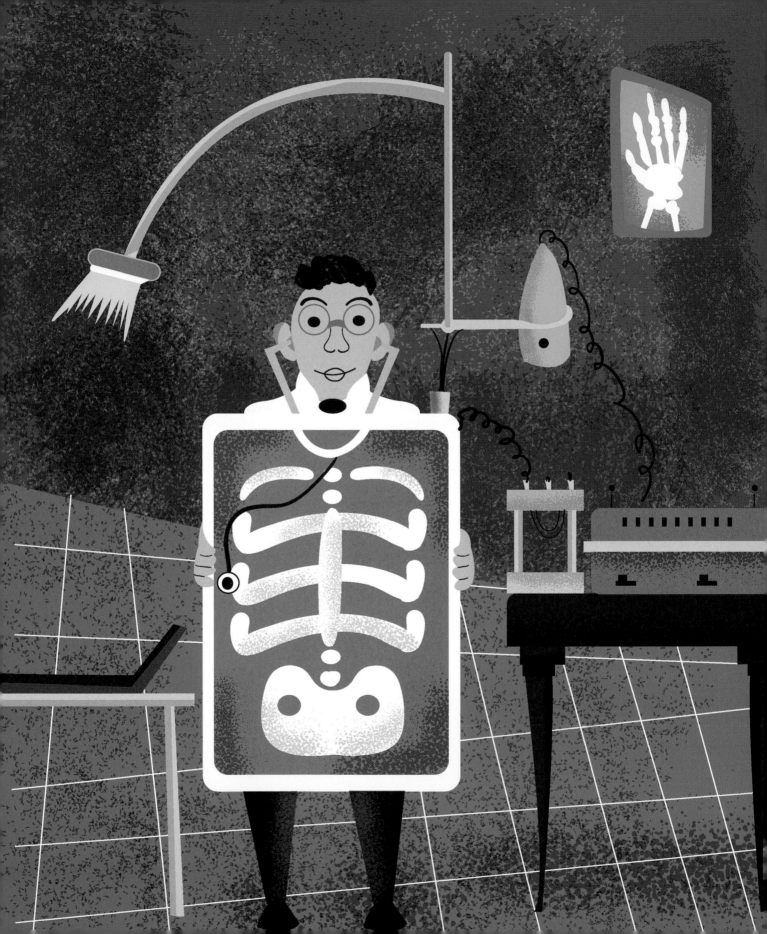

# ALAN L. HART

## (1890–1962, United States)

.....................

You can be **INVENTIVE** like Alan.

Alan L. Hart helped save thousands of lives as a doctor who pioneered the use of X-ray technology to detect illness in patients earlier than ever before.

> "I HAVE BEEN HAPPIER SINCE I MADE THIS CHANGE THAN I EVER HAVE IN MY LIFE."

# JOSEPHINE BAKER

**(1906–1975, United States/France)**

......................

You can be RESILIENT like Josephine.

Josephine Baker created a successful life for herself, even though no one helped her. She became a world-famous and beloved star who was also a spy, an activist, and a mom.

> "THE THINGS WE TRULY LOVE STAY WITH US ALWAYS, LOCKED IN OUR HEARTS AS LONG AS LIFE REMAINS."

All these people are LGBTQ+,
which means they have identities
as diverse as the rainbow.

CREATIVE

POETIC

INVENTIVE

BRAVE

ARTISTIC

DETERMINED

RESILIENT

You can be like them
by being YOU!

OUTSPOKEN

SMART

LOVING

INCLUSIVE

THOUGHTFUL

DARING

KIND

PEACE

# AUTHOR'S NOTE

History is brimming with incredible stories of LGBTQ+ heroes who helped shape our world. Parents and teachers can help children learn this history by teaching themselves more about these stories with the resources below and by sharing the information they learn in age-appropriate ways. When children see themselves reflected in the stories they hear, their idea of what they're capable of expands. When children see people different from themselves represented in the stories they hear, their idea of who can be a hero expands. No age is too young to learn about diverse historical figures.

## LEARN MORE:

GLBT Historical Society (glbthistory.org)

GLSEN (glsen.org)

History UnErased (unerased.org)

Making Gay History (makinggayhistory.com)

Queer Kid Stuff (queerkidstuff.com)

Quist (quistapp.com)

Teaching LGBTQ History (lgbtqhistory.org)

**SARAH PRAGER** is the author of *Queer, There, and Everywhere: 23 People Who Changed the World* and *Rainbow Revolutionaries: 50 LGBTQ+ People Who Made History*. She came out as lesbian when she was fourteen and feels grateful for her extended LGBTQ+ family and loves telling the stories of our shared history. She's written for the *New York Times*, *National Geographic*, *The Atlantic*, and many other publications about LGBTQ+ topics. Sarah lives with her wife and two children in Massachusetts.

**CHERYL "RAS" THUESDAY** is an illustrator originally from London and who grew up in New Jersey. Her illustrations are heavily influenced by her Caribbean and Asian heritage, and she's created artwork for various worldwide publications and companies. Cheryl lives in the Tri-State area.

POETIC BRAVE INVENTIVE ARTISTIC DETERMINED RE
LOVING THOUGHTFUL DARING POETIC BRAVE INVEN
OUTSPOKEN SMART INCLUSIVE LOVING THOUGHTFUL
RESILIENT KIND CREATIVE OUTSPOKEN SMART INC
INVENTIVE ARTISTIC DETERMINED RESILIENT KIN
THOUGHTFUL DARING POETIC BRAVE INVENTIVE ARTI
SMART INCLUSIVE LOVING THOUGHTFUL DARING PO
KIND CREATIVE OUTSPOKEN SMART INCLUSIVE LOVIN
DETERMINED RESILIENT KIND CREATIVE OUTSPOKEN
BRAVE INVENTIVE ARTISTIC DETERMINED RESILIENT
THOUGHTFUL DARING POETIC BRAVE INVENTIVE ARTI
SMART INCLUSIVE LOVING THOUGHTFUL DARING PO
KIND CREATIVE OUTSPOKEN SMART INCLUSIVE LOVIN
DETERMINED RESILIENT KIND CREATIVE OUTSPOKEN
BRAVE INVENTIVE ARTISTIC DETERMINED RESILIENT
THOUGHTFUL DARING POETIC BRAVE INVENTIVE ARTI
SMART INCLUSIVE LOVING THOUGHTFUL DARING PO
KIND CREATIVE OUTSPOKEN SMART INCLUSIVE LOVIN
DETERMINED RESILIENT KIND CREATIVE OUTSPOKEN
BRAVE INVENTIVE ARTISTIC DETERMINED RESILIENT